Teaching Little Fingers To Play More

By Leigh Kaplan

A follow-up book to
Teaching Little Fingers to Play

- Follows the John Thompson tradition
- Strengthens the skills learned in Teaching Little Fingers to Play
- Eases the transition into the Modern Course First Grade Book

Illustrations by Nick Gressle
Edited by David Engle

To access audio, visit:
www.halleonard.com/mylibrary

Enter Code
1776-8405-4204-3942

ISBN 978-1-4768-1381-3

Exclusively Distributed By
HAL•LEONARD®
7777 W. Bluemound Rd. P.O. Box 13819
Milwaukee, Wisconsin 53213

© 1997 by The Willis Music Co.
International Copyright Secured   All Rights Reserved

For all works contained herein:
Unauthorized copying, arranging, adapting, recording, Internet posting, public performance,
or other distribution of the printed or recorded music in this publication is an infringement of copyright.
Infringers are liable under the law.

Visit Hal Leonard Online at
www.halleonard.com

Note to Parents

The purpose of this book is to strengthen the skills introduced in John Thompson's *Teaching Little Fingers to Play*, thereby making the transition to the *First Grade Book* a comfortable one. Lyrics have been added to most of the pieces and they should be read before beginning the musical study. Guidelines accompany each piece, and it will be helpful if these are reviewed by parent and student together.

A most beneficial habit is for the parent to listen to the child perform his or her pieces at least once a week. This should be a regular occurrence where the parent's sole activity is attentive listening. The benefits to the child, both musical and emotional, cannot be overestimated.

To the Teacher

The purpose of this book is to strengthen the skills introduced in John Thompson's *Teaching Little Fingers to Play*, thereby making the transition to the *First Grade Book* a comfortable one.

Mr. Thompson's approach is to have the student gain considerable facility with both hands in a five-finger position before proceeding to other positions and techniques. Rather than introducing new concepts, *Teaching Little Fingers To Play More* applies Mr. Thompson's approach to new pieces. Both hands stay in the five-finger positions, but new juxtapositions are added. Half steps are used occasionally, requiring that a finger play more than one key. Some easy two-note chords (also called harmonic intervals) are introduced, thus preparing the student for their more challenging use in the *First Grade Book*.

In *Teaching Little Fingers To Play More,* all previously learned terms, principles and techniques are employed in new contexts in order to reinforce skills. Generally the pieces are longer than those in *Teaching Little Fingers to Play*, thereby furthering concentration and stamina.

Please note that there is less fingering indicated than in *Teaching Little Fingers to Play*, thereby encouraging the student to read by note and/or interval.

Best wishes to both student and teacher for a wonderful musical adventure in *Teaching Little Fingers to Play More*!

Contents

The Swing 4
Comin' Through the Rye 6
The Pet Parade 7
Shall We Waltz? 8
On the Contrary 9
The Top 10
Halloween Fest 11
My Shadow 12
Pat, My Cat 14
Waltz Without Words 16
The New Birthday Song 17
Outer Space 18
The Circus 20
A Computer 22
Go Tell Aunt Rhody 24
Two Friends and a Secret 25
'Tis a Gift to Be Simple 26
Lightly Row 27
Swanee River (duet) 28
Glossary of Terms and Symbols 30
Certificate 31

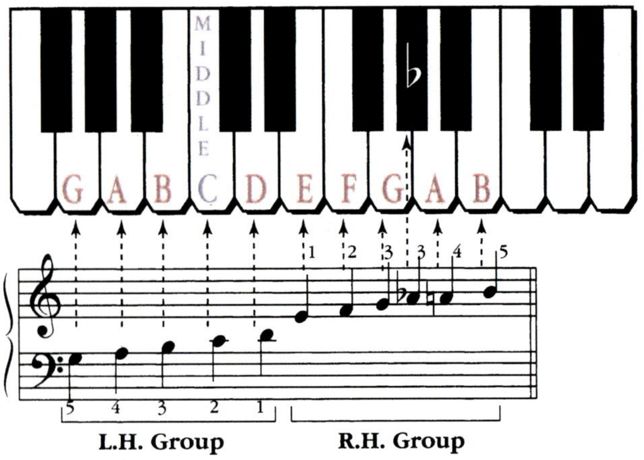

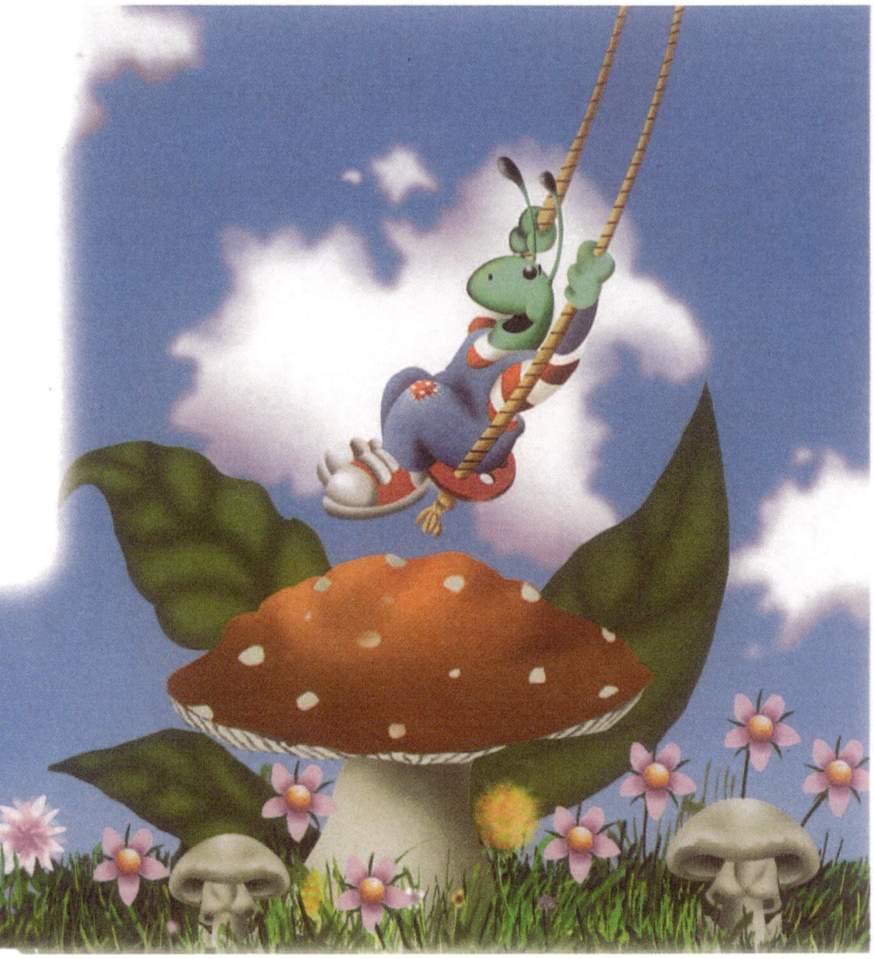

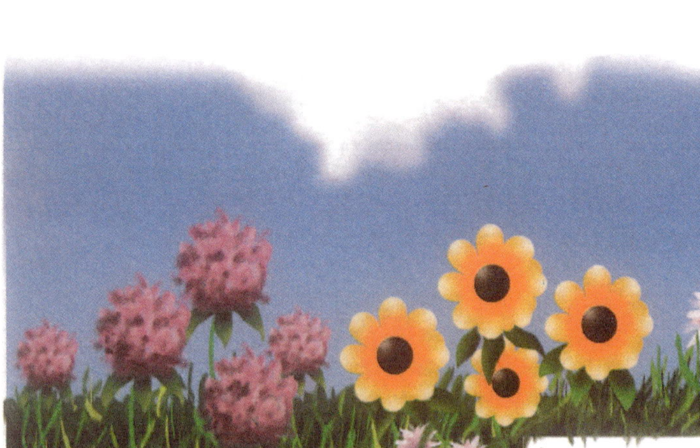

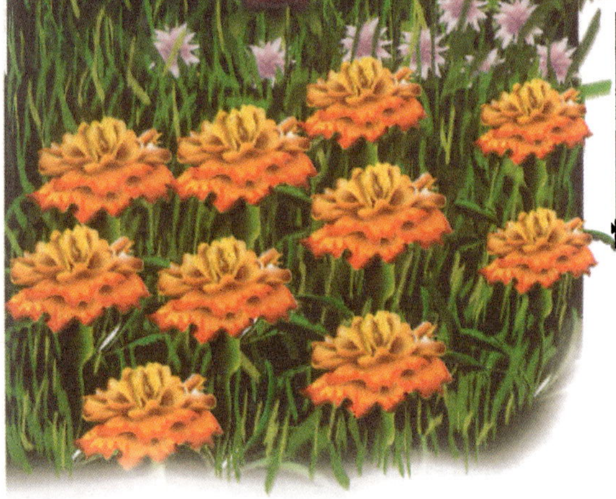

MIDDLE
G A B C D E F G A B
1 2 3 3 4 5
5 4 3 2 1
L.H. Group
R.H. Group

What is the one accidental that we find in this piece?
D.C. al Fine is the abbreviation for the Italian words *Da Capo al Fine*, which mean to return to the beginning (*Capo*) and stop at the *Fine* (end).

The Swing

1/2

Poem by Robert Louis Stevenson

Smoothly
How do you like to go up in a swing?
Till I look down on the gar - den green,
Up in the air so blue.
Down on the roof so brown.

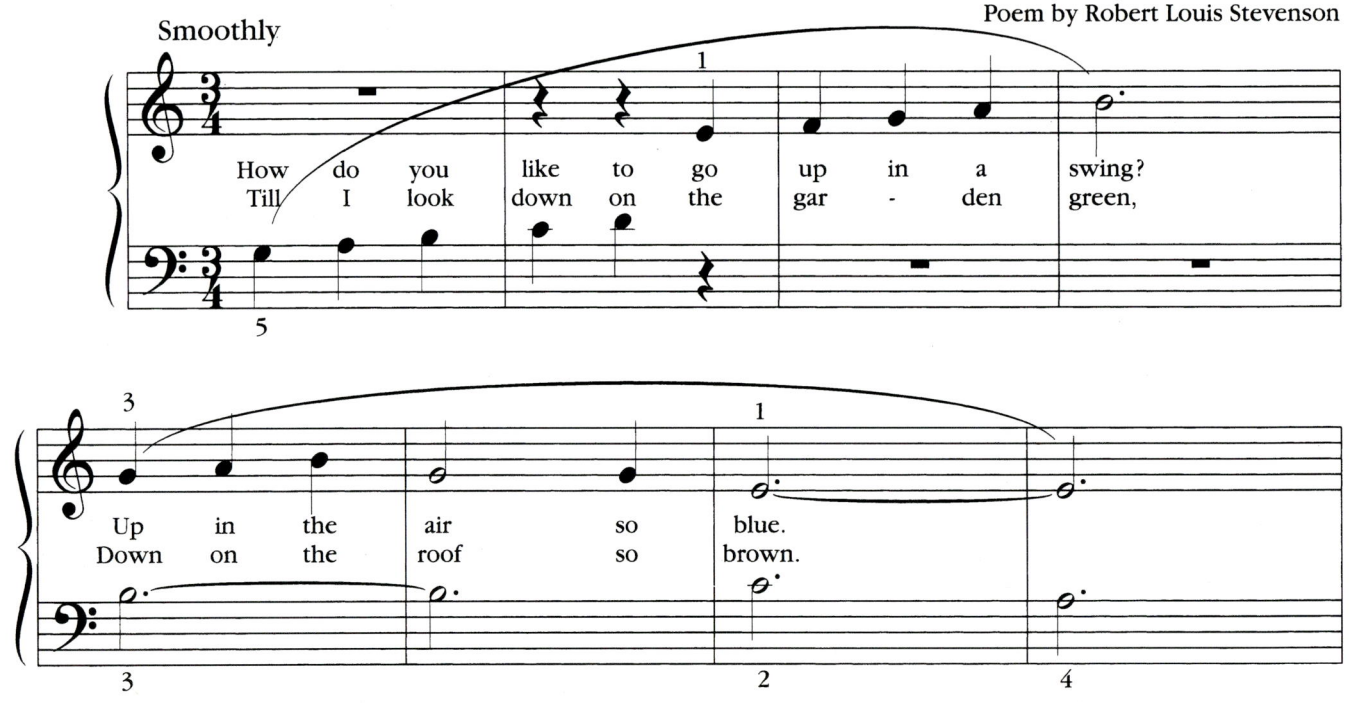

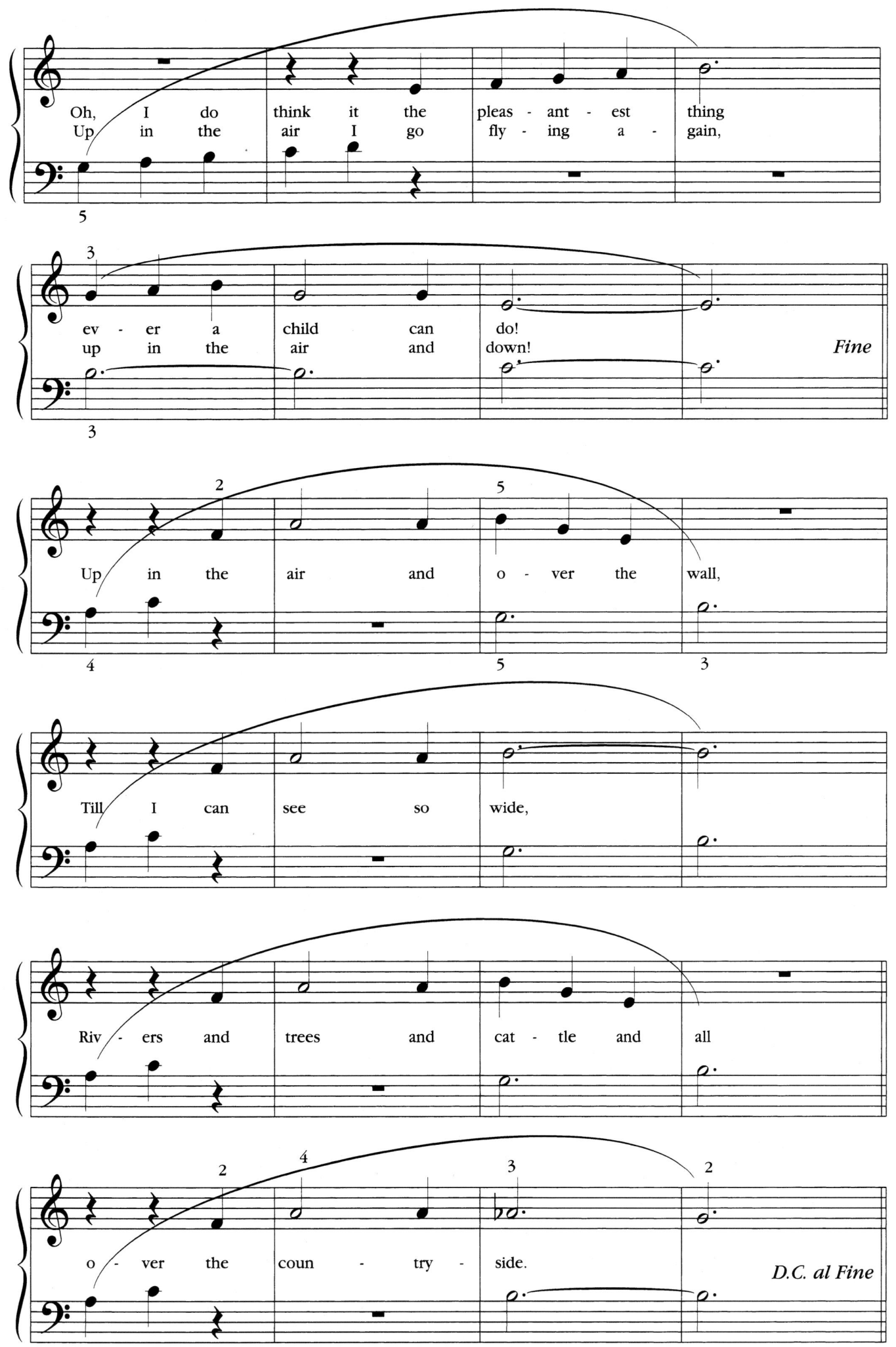

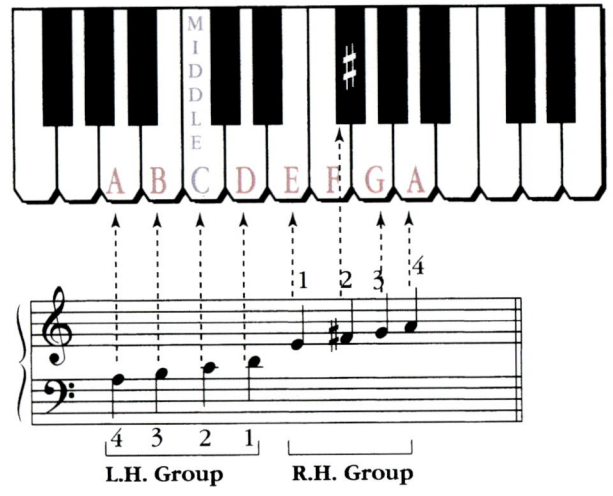

PREPARATION – Practice clapping these two rhythms as you count aloud: 3/4 ♩ ♩ | ♩ ♩ ♩ | and | ♩ ♩ ♩ | ♩ ♩ ♩ ||

How many F-Sharps are there in this piece? _____

Are there any F-Naturals? _____

Comin' Through the Rye

3/4

Medium speed

Scottish Folk Song

Remember that the time value of an eighth note ♪ is half as long as that of a quarter note.

An eighth rest 𝄾 receives half a count, just like an eighth note.

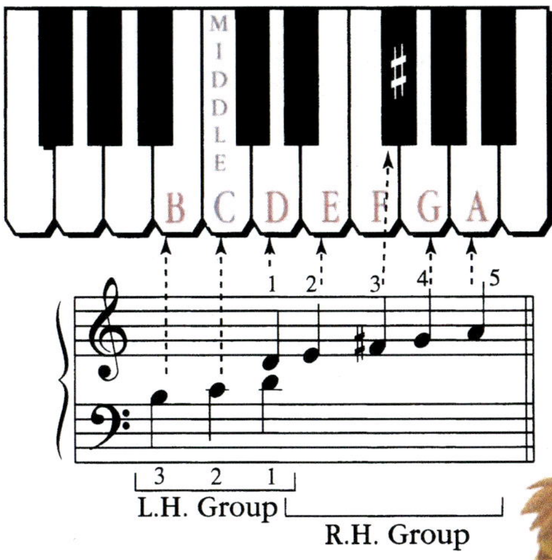
MIDDLE
B C D E F G A
1 2 3 4 5
3 2 1
L.H. Group
R.H. Group

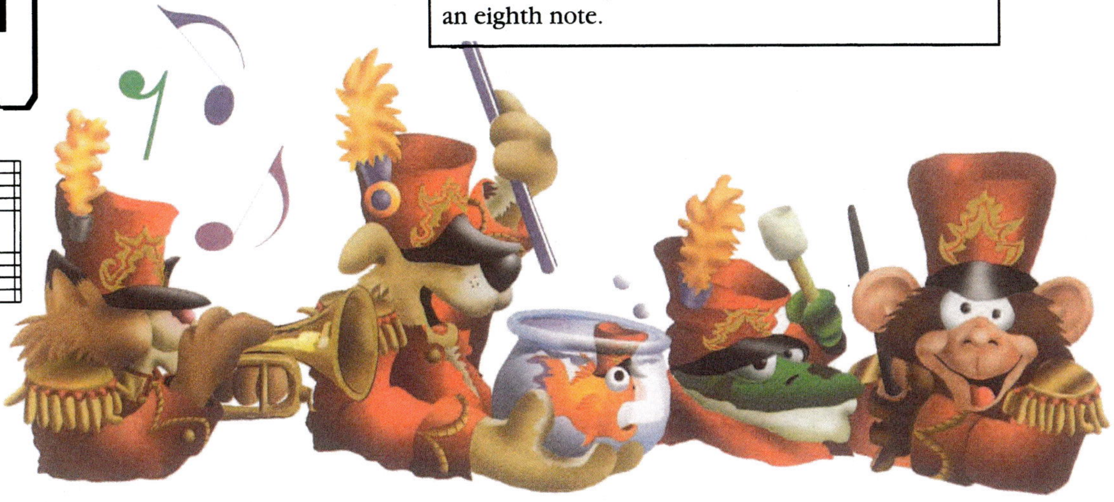

The Pet Parade

5/6

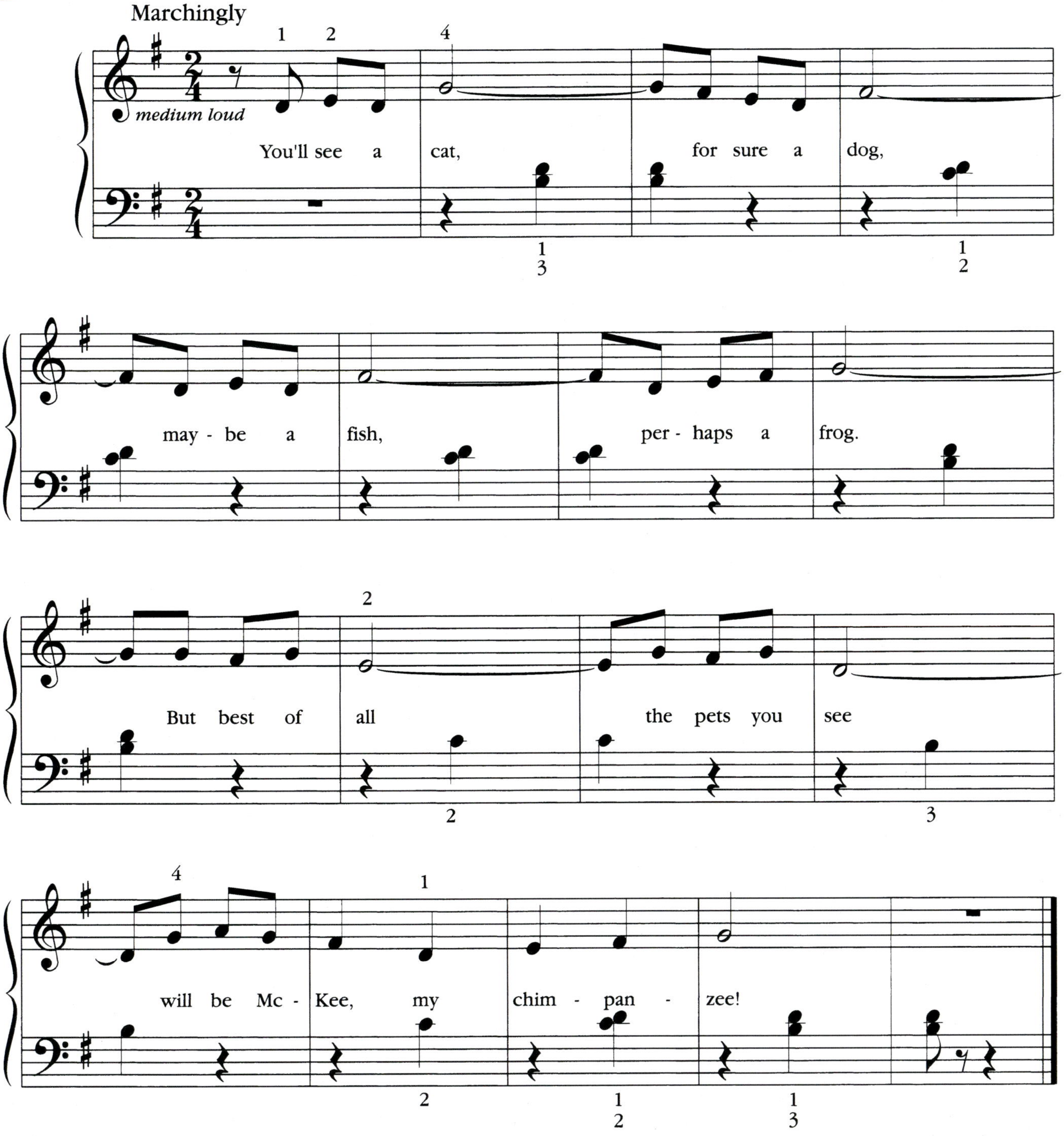
Marchingly
medium loud
You'll see a cat, for sure a dog,
may - be a fish, per - haps a frog.
But best of all the pets you see
will be Mc - Kee, my chim - pan - zee!

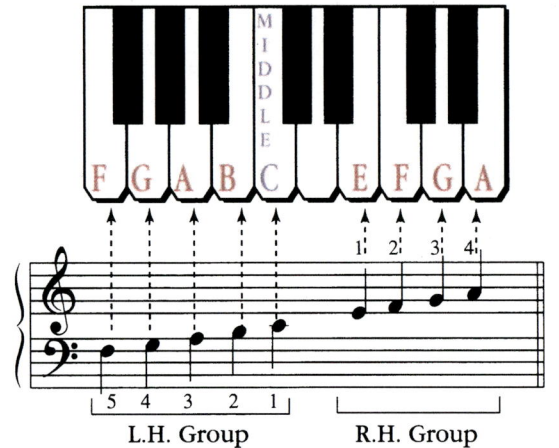

MELODY - The melody is the most important element in music.

In this piece the left hand plays the melody and the right hand plays the **accompaniment**.

Which hand should be playing louder? _____

An accent > means to give extra stress.

Shall We Waltz?

🔊 7/8

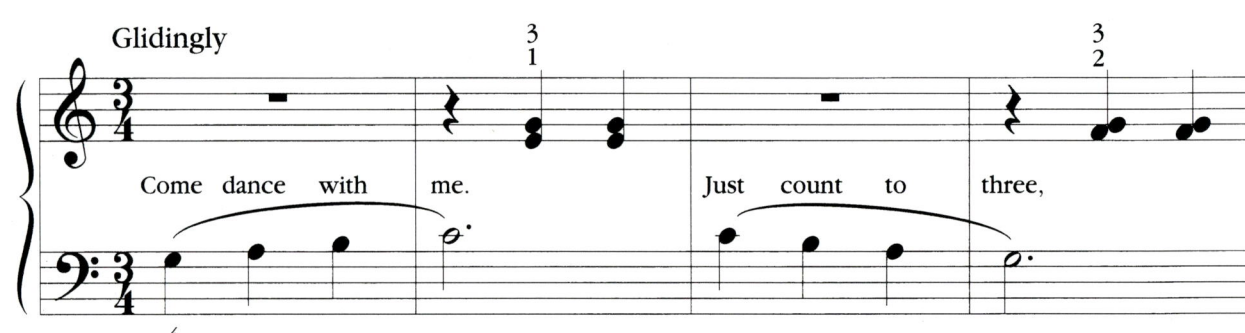

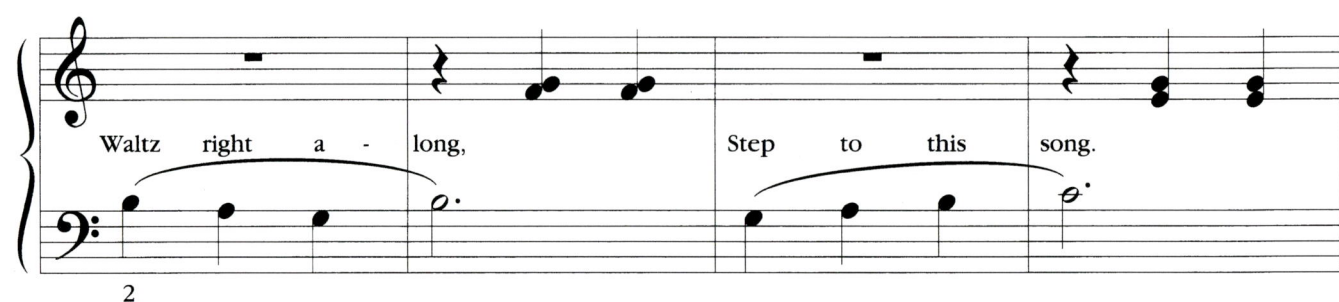

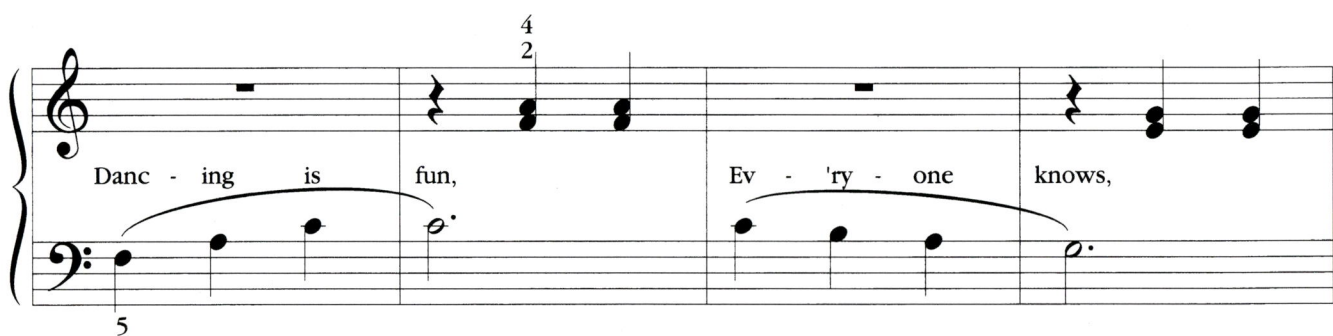

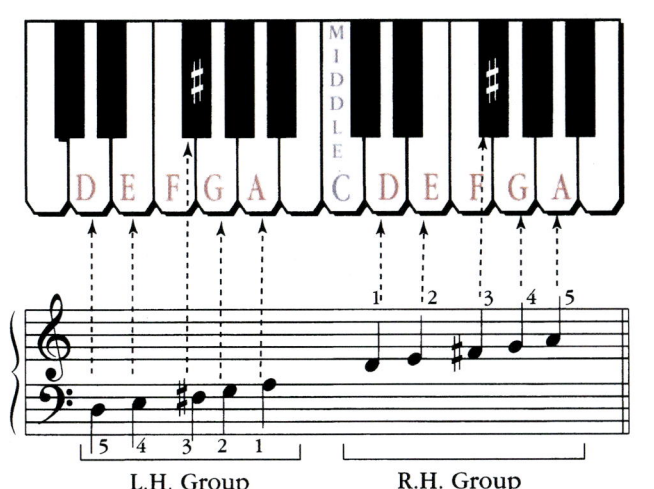

To be contrary means to take an opposite point of view. In music, when one voice goes in the opposite direction of another, it is called contrary motion. How many times does the right hand make a contrary response to the left hand? _____

What do two friends in this piece finally agree upon? _____

In which measure does this happen? _____

 9/10

On The Contrary

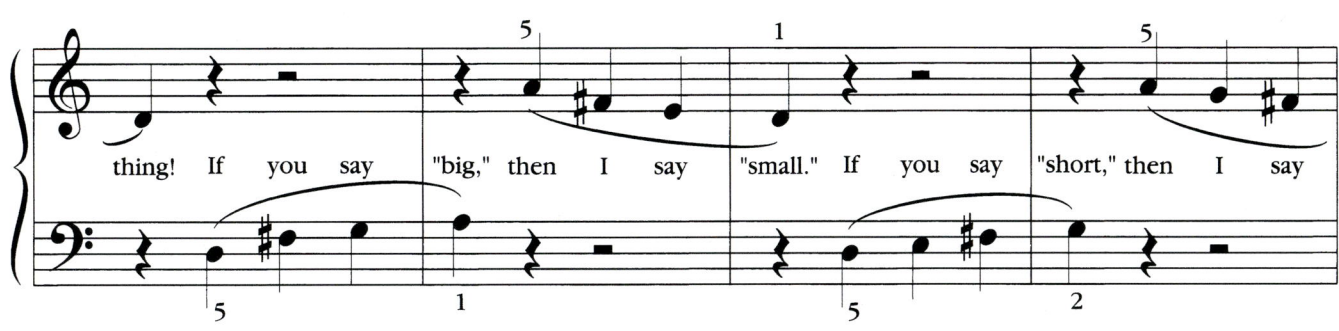

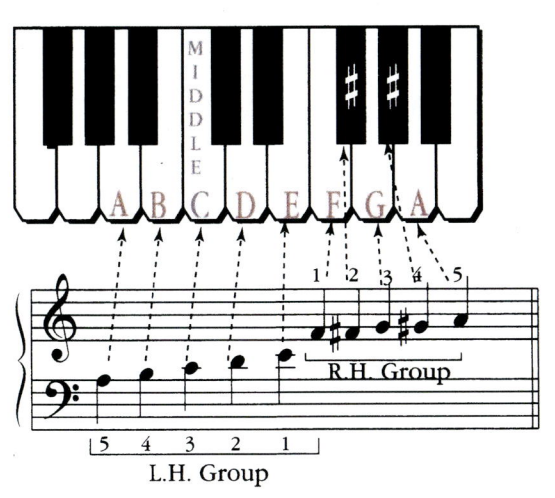

The natural sign in measures 3, 5, 11 and 13 is not necessary, but it serves to remind us that the bar line has cancelled the written-in accidental in the previous measure.

Halloween Fest

🔊 13/14

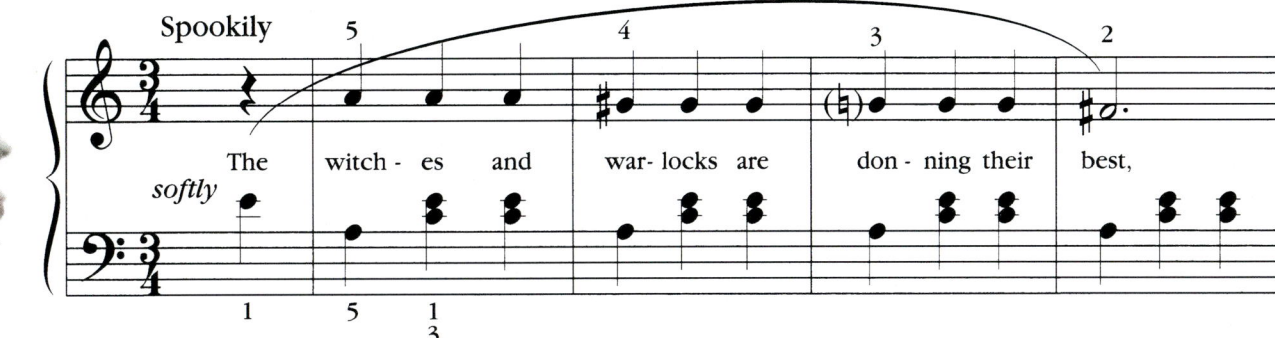

Spookily / softly
The witch- es and war- locks are don- ning their best,

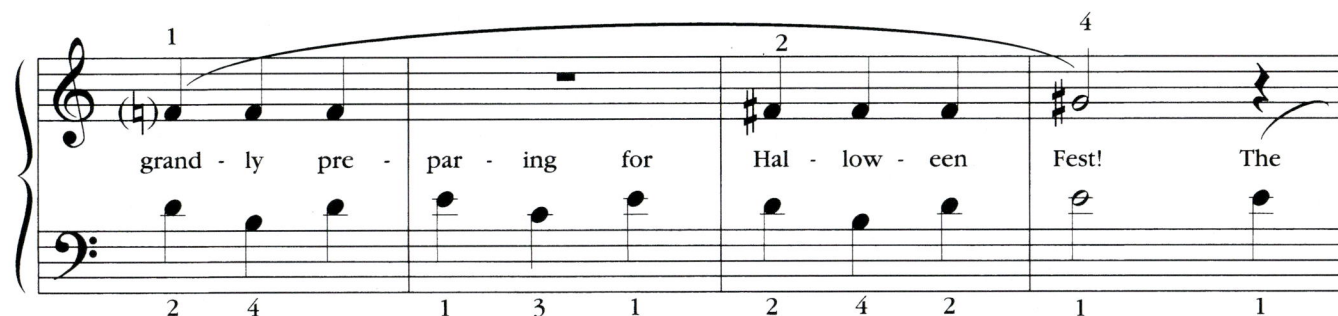

grand- ly pre- par- ing for Hal- low- een Fest! The

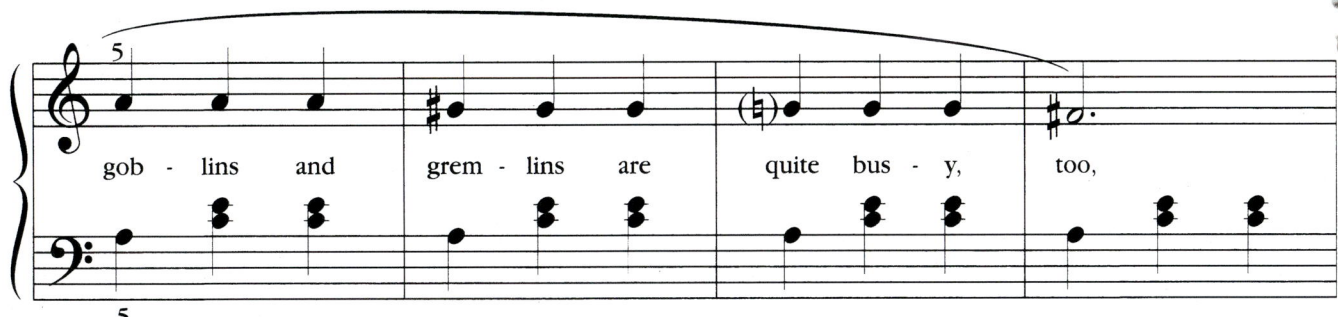

gob- lins and grem- lins are quite bus- y, too,

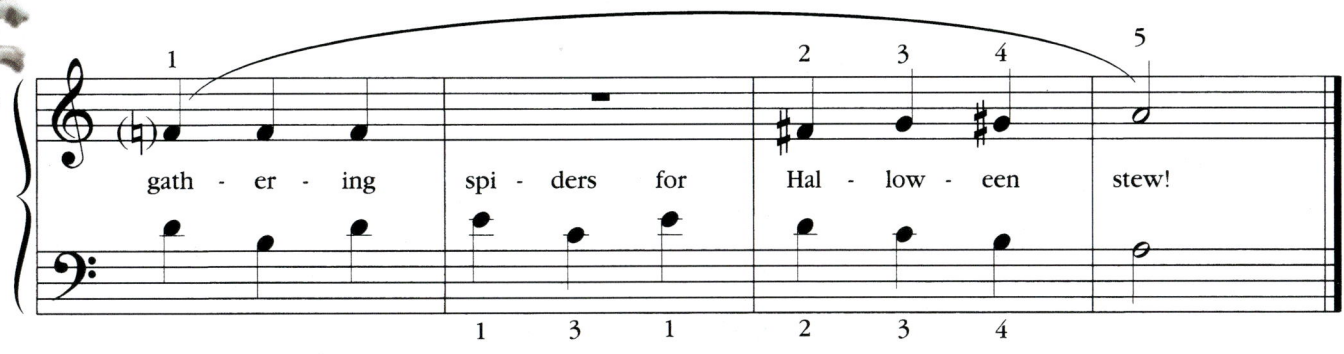

gath- er- ing spi- ders for Hal- low- een stew!

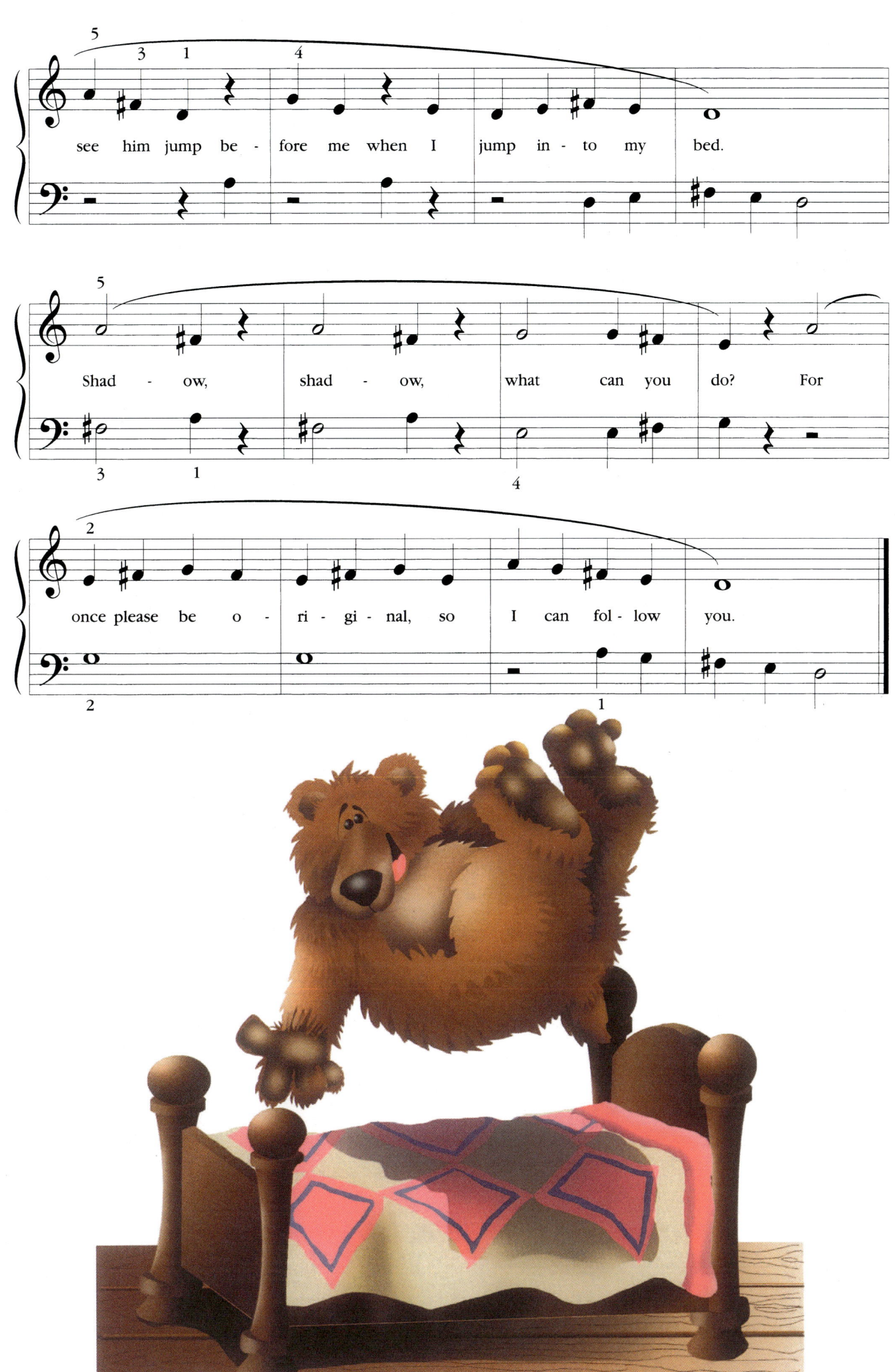

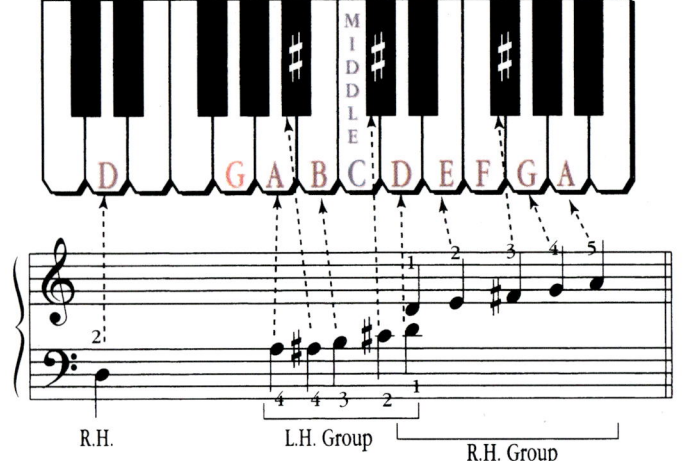

Name the sharps in PAT, MY CAT. _____ , _____ , _____ .
Where does the opening melody return? Measure _____
For how many measures is it exactly like the beginning? _____

Remember that measure number one is always the first complete measure.

🔊 17/18

Pat, My Cat

Purringly

loud

I have a cat, her name is Pat, and she is rath-er fat! So when

Pat, my cat, sat on my hat, I said, "Oh no, oh no!" But

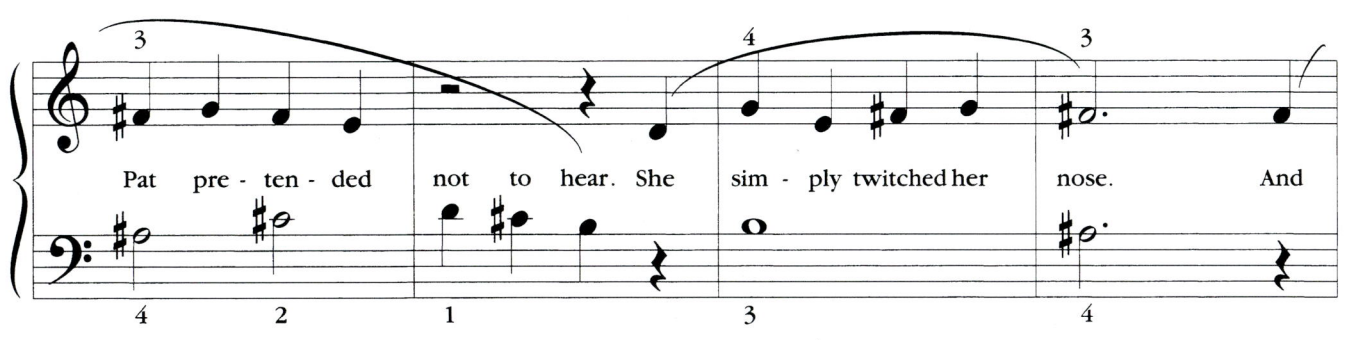
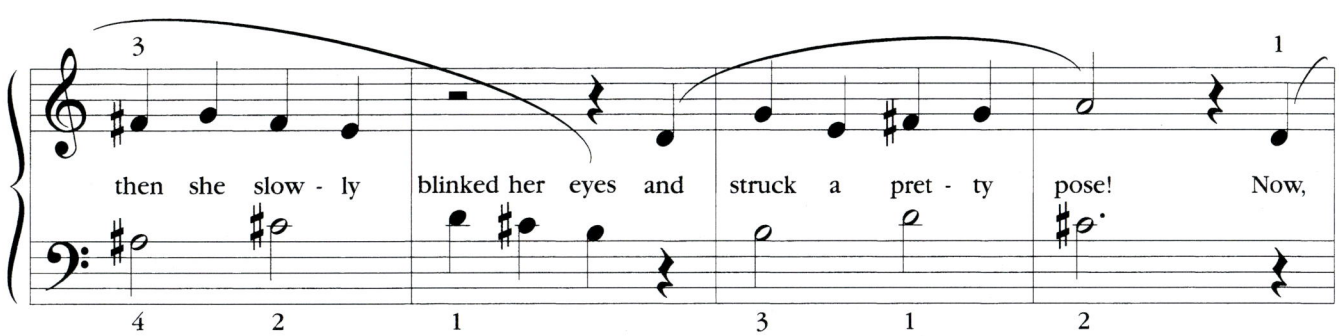

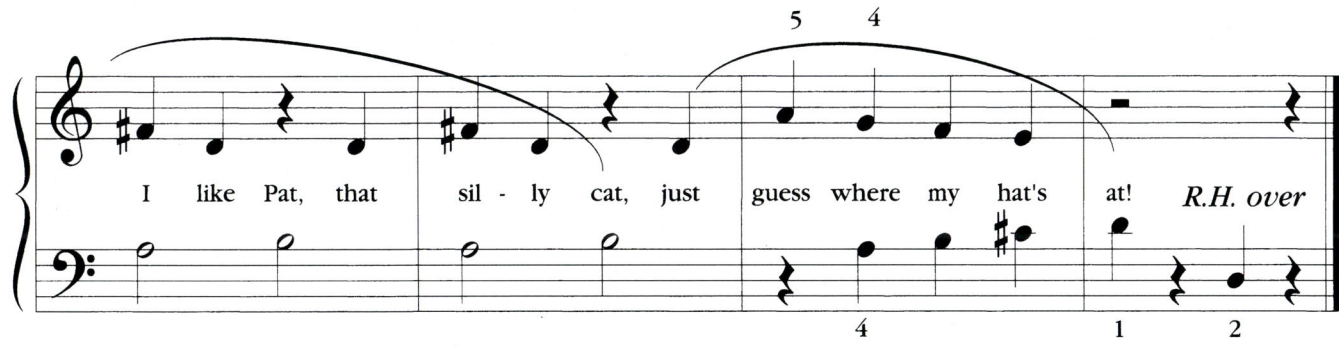

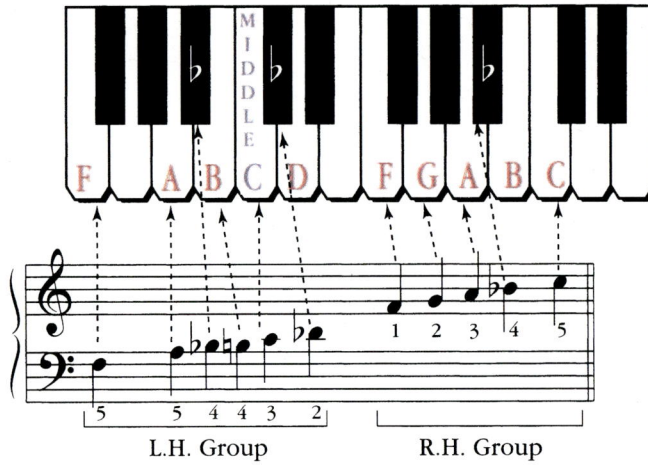

How many pairs of measures are exactly the same as those in the broken line box? _____

Waltz Without Words

🔊 19/20

Find the measure where the right hand has three beats of rest while the left hand has four beats of rest. _____
What note does the key signature tell you to sharp? _____

A Computer ? 🔊 27/28

Swingingly

medium loud

Have you ev-er seen Grand-ma's writ-ing ma-chine? I think it is aw-ful-ly old. It clicks and it jumps when I

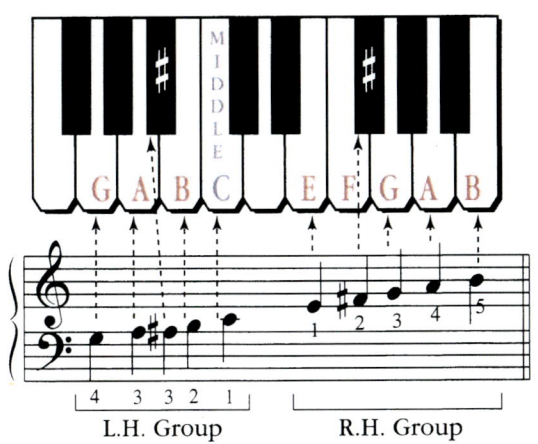

THE MELODY is the part you can sing or hum. In this piece, why do the hands take turns playing the melody?

Two Friends and a Secret

🔊 31/32

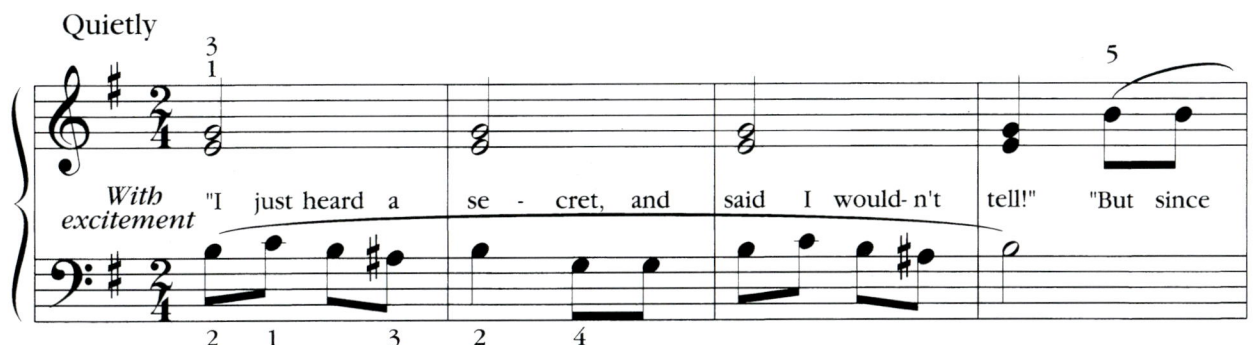

Quietly / With excitement
"I just heard a se - cret, and said I would - n't tell!" "But since

I can keep a se - cret, too, you might tell me as well!" "Then just

lean a lit - tle clos - er and guess what I will say." "You'll say

ab - so - lute - ly noth - ing, you're not giv - ing it a - way!"

Swanee River
Duet (Secondo)

Stephen Foster

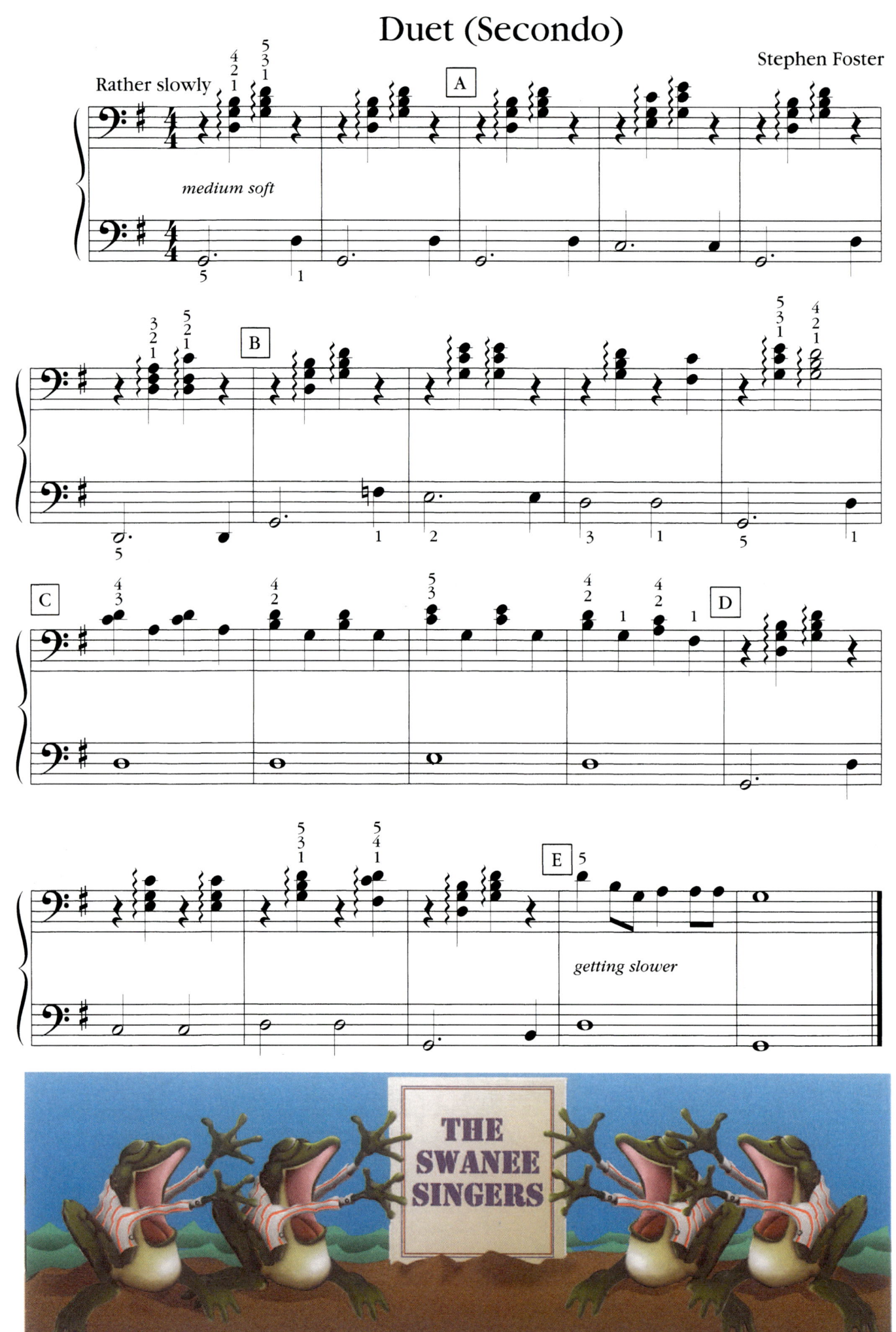

MIDDLE C
G A B C D E F G A
R.H. Group
L.H. Group

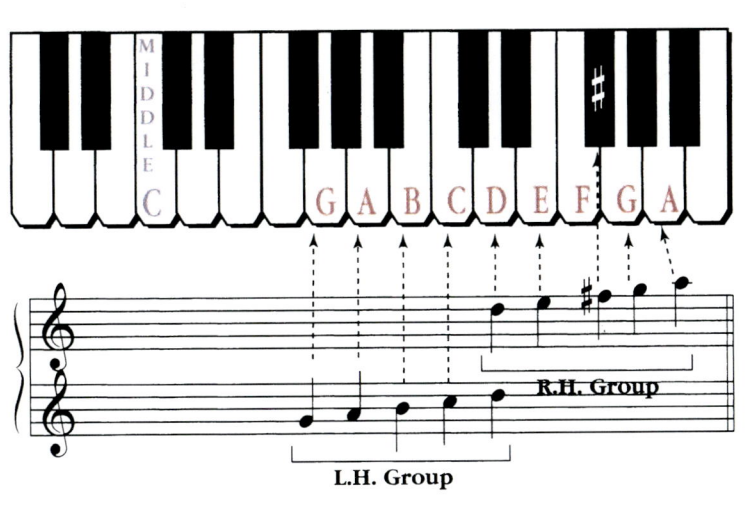

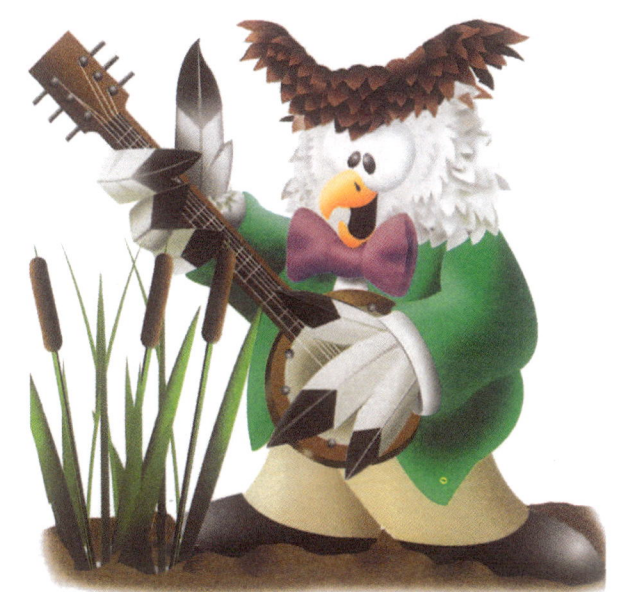

Swanee River

(Primo)

37/38

Stephen Foster

Rather slowly
A
1
2
with a singing tone
medium loud
B
C
D
E
getting slower

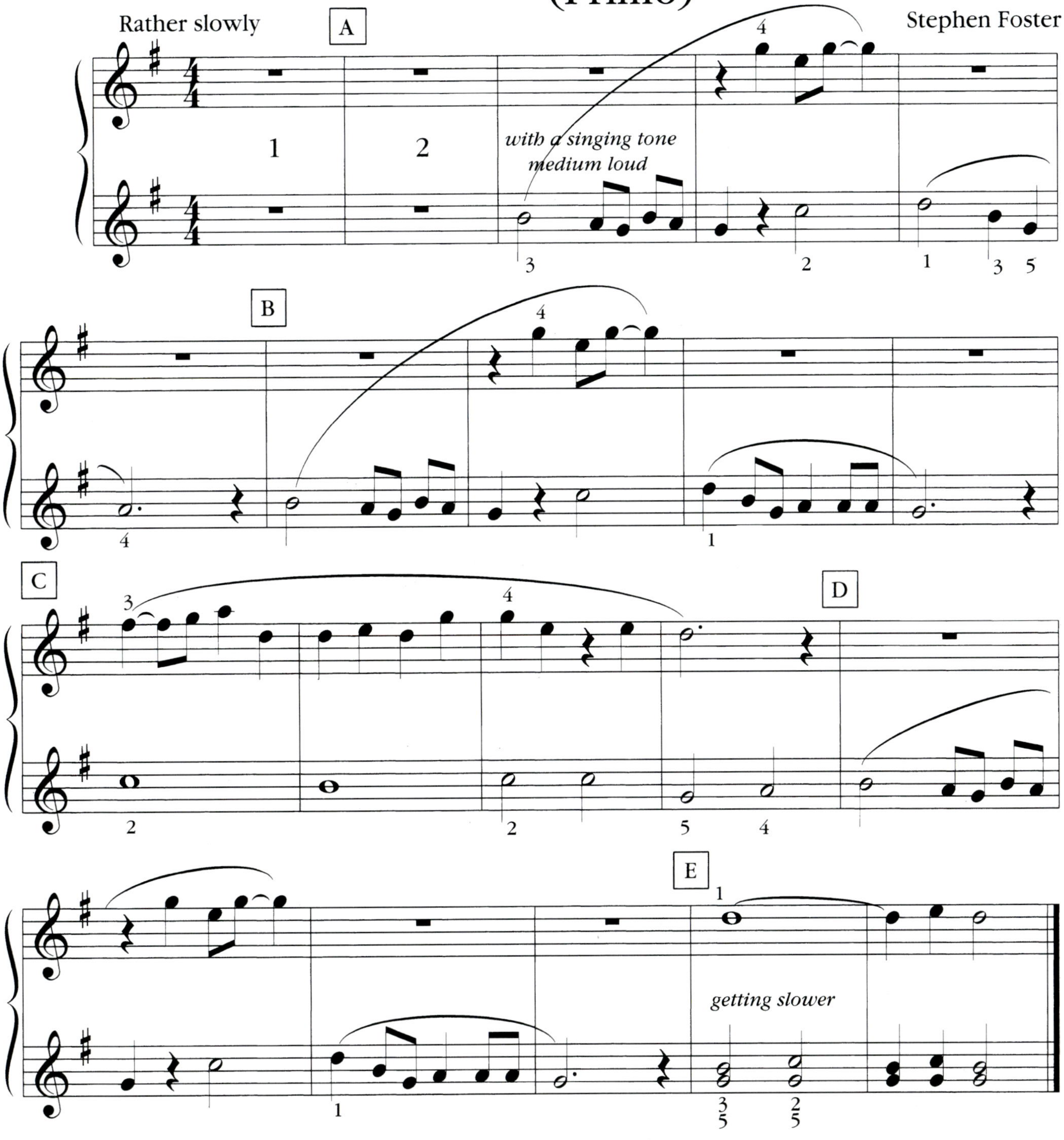

Glossary of Terms and Symbols

TERM	DEFINITION
> Accent	Give extra stress to the note.
Canon	A melody that imitates another. A round.
Coda	A short ending section.
D.C. al Fine	Repeat from the beginning and play to the word "fine".
Eighth Rest	1/2 count of silence.
Fermata	Hold the note for longer than its value.
Fine	The end.
♭ Flat	Play the very closest (usually black) key to the left.
Harmonic Interval	Two keys played together.
Introduction	A short musical phrase before the main part of the piece.
Melody	The part you can hum or sing. Sometimes it has words.
♮ Natural	It cancels a sharp or flat.
Primo	The treble part of a duet.
Secondo	The bass part of a duet.
♯ Sharp	Play the very closest (usually black) key to the right.

Certificate Of Merit

This certifies that

....

has successfully completed

Teaching Little Fingers To Play More

....
Teacher

....
Date

Leigh Kaplan

Leigh Kaplan began her piano study at the age of eight—her first book being John Thompson's *Teaching Little Fingers to Play*—and holds Baccalaureate and Masters Degrees in Piano Performance from the University of Southern California, where she was a full scholarship recipient.

Ms. Kaplan, who frequently appears as a solo recitalist and ensemble player, has been a guest artist with the Boston Pops and has lectured at universities and on various prestigious platforms, including the Smithsonian Institute. She taught piano at Citrus College in Covina, California, and later served as Assistant Professor of Music at El Camino College in Torrance, California.

Leigh Kaplan's piano solos and piano duets are published by The Willis Music Company, and her classical and jazz recordings are on the Cambria label. She and her husband currently make their home in Arroyo Grande, California.

Nick Gressle

Nick Gressle is a freelance illustrator. He received his Baccalaureate degree in Graphic Design from Northern Kentucky University in 1988, and has since published several of his illustrations in a variety of print and interactive media.

Teaching Little Fingers To Play was Mr. Gressle's first major work for The Willis Music Company.

Mr. Gressle maintains his studio in Mt. Washington, Ohio.